Projection Art for Kids

Projection Art
FOR KIDS

MURALS & PAINTING PROJECTS FOR KIDS OF ALL AGES

by Linda Buckingham
Illustrations by Marian Robinson

Hartley
&Marks
PUBLISHERS

Published by
Hartley & Marks Publishers Inc.
P.O. Box 147   3661 West Broadway
Point Roberts, WA   Vancouver, BC
98281   V6R 2B8

Photographs by Ken Mayer
Photographs on page 14, 15, 19–21, 66–69, 71–75 by Linda Buckingham
Photographs on page 94–97 by Hydeman Art of Photography

Design and composition by John McKercher
Cover design by Diane McIntosh
Printed in Hong Kong

LIBRARY OF CONGRESS CATALOGING-IN-PUBLICATION DATA

Buckingham, Linda
    Projection art for kids : painting big made easy / by Linda Buckingham ;
illustrations by Marian Robinson.
        p. cm.
    Includes index.
    Summary: Explores the tools and techniques of projection art, a way of turning nearly
any printed image into a painting of any size.
    ISBN 0-88179-197-0
    1. Handicraft—Juvenile literature.   2. Projection art—Juvenile literature.   3. Mural
painting and decorating—Technique—Juvenile literature. [1. Handicraft. 2. Mural painting
and decoration—Technique. 3. Painting.]   I. Robinson, Marian, ill.   II. Title.

TT160.B8587   2002
751.73—dc21   2002024114

To my daughter, Dana,
for inspiration, feedback, love, laughter
and just plain hard work.

Paint Pen Projects

Contents

Comic Relief
22

Guard Frog
26

Butterfly World
29

Dig This
32

Best Laid Plans
34

Furious
38

Easy Rider
43

Hanging Out
46

Mermaid
49

Teddy Bears' Picnic
52

Pleasantville Playmat
56

Projection Stenciling Projects

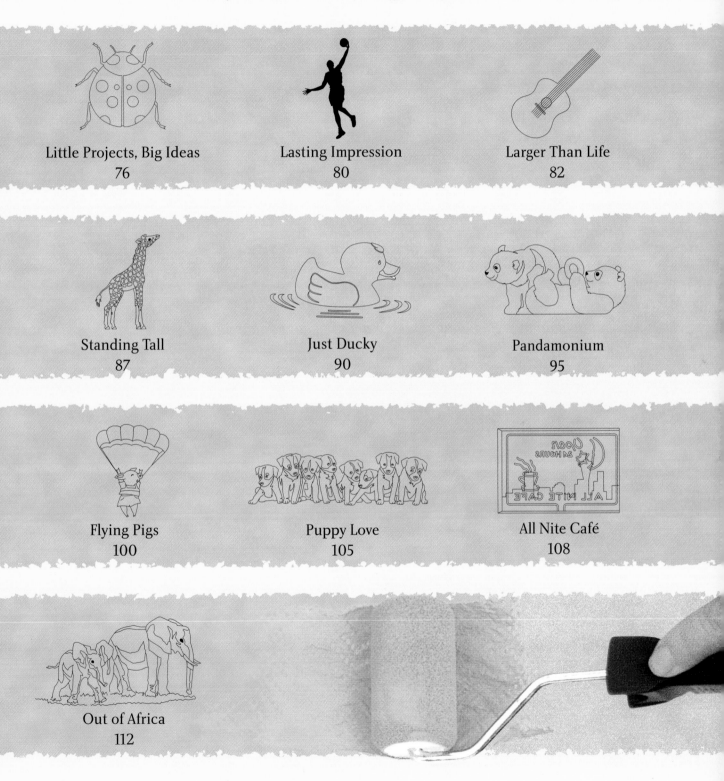

Foreword

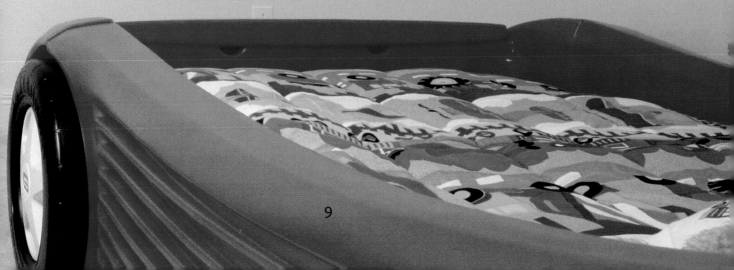

WE ALL BEGIN as artists. As babies we use our pudgy fingers to draw designs in our food. As toddlers we delight in using sticks to make our mark in the sand. As small children we discover crayons, pencils, and paints, and our fingers itch to experiment with these on any and every surface. The joy and excitement of creating our own artwork is like no other!

But sadly, for most of us, our term as an artist is short lived. Somewhere along the way art is transformed from adventuresome play to art*work*, a subject in school. Our favorite pastime becomes study, and we worry that our efforts won't measure up.

Overnight, it seems, art changes from being an exhilarating form of self-expression to an exercise over which we agonize. Just hand any adult a pencil or a crayon and ask him to draw a picture. You will see what I mean.

Projection art allows anyone to succeed as an artist. In the hands of the young, it is an exciting and empowering tool. As for the rest of us, it is as though Peter Pan has taken our hand and allowed us entry into a world long forgotten.

What is Projection Art?

PROJECTION ART is a technique that allows you to turn almost any printed image into a painting of any size. It requires no special skill other than the ability to trace.

Have you ever been handed a pencil and asked to draw a person? If you are like me, your face flushed, your hand froze, and you ended up drawing a very primitive stick figure in an attempt to laugh off the insecurity you felt about your artistic abilities.

Now imagine – you, the artist, producing beautiful paintings, from small panels to large wall murals. That's the power of Projection Art.

This book teaches two types of Projection Art – Paint Pen Projection Art and Projection Stenciling. With both painting techniques you need a picture and some way of enlarging it or transferring it from the printed page to your painting surface. The picture can be taken from this or any other book, adapted from a comic book or magazine, or drawn from your own imagination.

The type of art you are reproducing will determine which method of Projection Art you choose. If the image has an outline, as many cartoons and ink drawings do, you'll use the paint pen method of painting. If your image is comprised of blocks of color, like some photographs or paintings, you'll want to use the stenciling method.

Paint Pen Projection Art and Projection Stenciling both require enlarging and tracing an image, but each one has a very different painting method. For this reason, once enlarging and tracing are discussed, the book is divided into two sections, one for paint pen projects and the other for stenciling projects. No matter which method you choose you can't help but impress yourself!

NOTE TO PARENTS

Because of safety concerns surrounding the use of craft knives and spray adhesive, Projection Stenciling projects should be restricted to older children. This does not mean, however, that young children

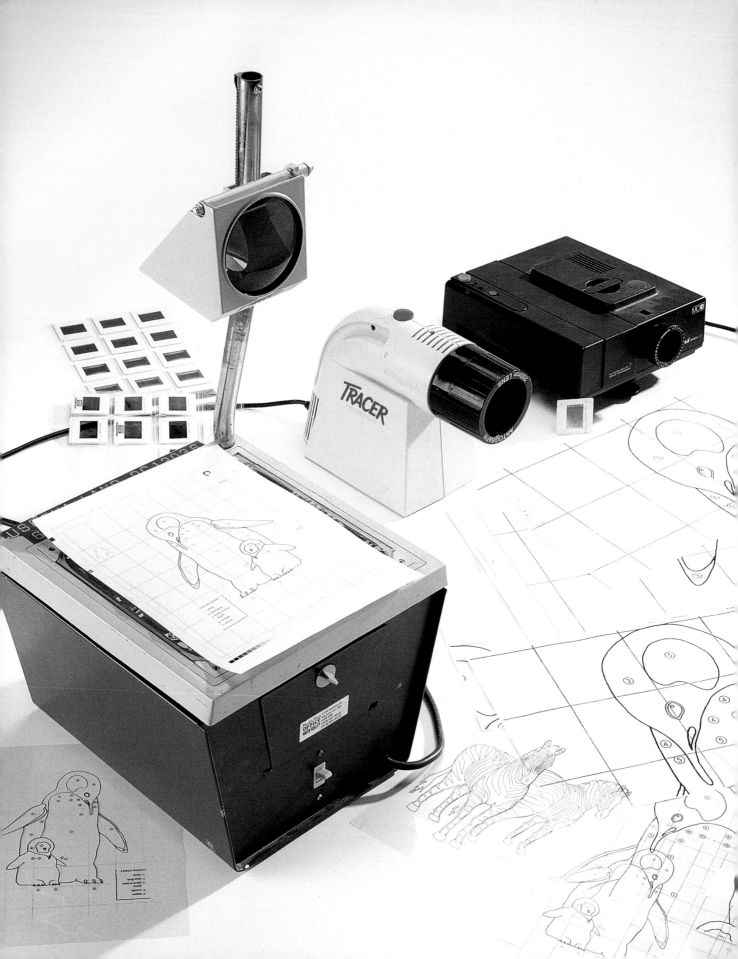

cannot be involved in the painting process. They can participate in the selection of projects for their room and can help with actually painting the walls. Because stenciling is a "dry paint" technique, even a very young child can paint in designated areas as long as you load his paint applicator and off-load the excess paint before he begins stenciling. You can be sure your child will take great pride in any contribution he has made to the artwork.

As soon as children are old enough to trace they can do Projection Art projects with paint pens. I recommend children practice on paper before undertaking wall murals, and I'm sure you will too! If you do the tracing and the projecting for them, even very young children can get involved in Projection Art. By projecting and tracing your drawings onto large sheets of paper you can create a giant coloring book for them to color in with crayons, paint pens, or color washes.

ENLARGING AND TRANSFERRING YOUR IMAGE

For both types of Projection Art, Paint Pen Projection and Projection Stenciling, you need a method of enlarging your image or transferring it from the printed page onto your painting surface.

There are three ways to enlarge a design for stenciling – photocopying, using the grid system, or using a light projector. If your project is small, photocopying may be the best option. If the project is large and you don't have access to a projector, the grid system is the way to go.

PHOTOCOPYING FOR PROJECTION STENCILING

Use a photocopier to enlarge your design to the size you want it painted. Apply repositionable or stencil spray glue (adult supervision required) to the back of the photocopy and position the photocopy over the shiny side of a piece of freezer paper. Spray the back side (non-shiny side) of the freezer paper with stencil adhesive and position it on your painting surface. The freezer paper acts as a stencil material (see Stencil Material page 62). Your design is now ready to be cut out and then stenciled.

PHOTOCOPYING FOR PAINT PEN PROJECTION ART

Use a photocopier to print out your design at the desired size. Transfer the photocopied design onto your painting surface by placing carbon paper or transfer paper under the photocopy before taping your photocopy in place.

Use a pen or pencil to trace over your photocopied design. Be sure to press hard enough to leave a clear impression from the carbon or transfer paper.

GRID SYSTEM

Draw horizontal and vertical lines in a grid over your picture.

For Paint Pen Projection Art, draw a bigger grid on the surface you are painting. Then, square by square, copy the picture onto the big grid. Use a pencil or a chalk pencil to draw the grid and the artwork so that you can erase the lines once your painting is finished.

For Projection Stenciling projects, draw your bigger grid and your enlarged artwork on freezer paper using a permanent felt marker. Use one color of marker to draw the grid and another color to draw the artwork.

LIGHT PROJECTOR

The easiest light projector to use is the Tracer by Artograph. It is a lightweight projector powered by a 100-watt light bulb. To use it, place the viewer (the opening on the bottom of the projector) over your picture and turn out the lights in the room. The darker the room, the sharper and brighter your image will appear. If your picture is larger than 5″× 5″, you may wish to reduce the picture on a photocopier rather than projecting it in sections. The Tracer will enlarge your drawing up to twelve times its original size. For small projects you can use the Junior Tracer by Artograph. Its viewing size is 3″× 3″.

Overhead projectors are also great for enlarging your artwork. They are more expensive than Tracers, but have the advantage of allowing you to work in a well-lit room. To use an overhead projector you need to photocopy your picture onto a piece of clear plastic called a transparency. Transparencies are available from office supply stores and photocopy shops.

No matter which type of projector you use, the size of the projected image will depend on the placement of the projector. The closer the projector is to the painting surface, the smaller the image will appear; the further away it is, the larger the image.

TRACING YOUR IMAGE

Project your image onto the wall or surface you are painting. Once you have adjusted the size of the image and brought it into focus, make sure your pattern doesn't shift. If you are using an overhead projector, tape your transparency onto the bed of the projector.

For Paint Pen Projection

Use paint pens to trace the enlarged image directly onto your painting surface. If your painting surface is in an awkward position for projecting, first project the image onto paper and then transfer the image where you want to paint it using carbon or transfer paper.

For Projection Stenciling

Use painter's tape to mark the outer dimensions of your project.

Cut freezer paper to cover the full length and height of your image and then some. One piece of freezer paper may be enough if your projected design is not very big.

Lay your freezer paper on the floor, shiny side down. Making sure the room is well ventilated and the floor is protected with newspaper, spray each strip of paper with stencil adhesive. Let the freezer paper sit for a few minutes before applying it to your wall. NOTE: *This step must be done by an adult, or by an older child with the help of an adult.*

Stick the freezer paper to the wall where the projected image appears. Lay one sheet at a time by holding the paper vertically, slightly away from the wall. Stick the freezer paper on the wall, working from top to bottom. Once you have the first sheet in place, line up the second and continue until you have covered the entire area on which the image appears. Use painter's tape around the top, bottom, and sides of the freezer paper to make sure the paper doesn't shift.

Use Scotch tape to cover the seams where the sheets of paper meet.

Using a fine tip permanent felt marker trace your projected image onto the freezer paper.

NOTE: *If your room is too small to project your image to the size you desire, project and trace your artwork in a larger room and then move the traced pattern to the small room for cutting and painting.*

Paint Pen Projection Art

JUST LIKE A LITTLE KID in a new candy store, I couldn't contain my excitement when I discovered paint pens. Why all the enthusiasm? From small craft projects to large-scale murals, decorative painting has never been so easy – no paint to spill, no brushes to wash, no brush technique to master.

If you want to earn bonus points on your next school project, or make a sign to advertise your lemonade sale, paint pens may become your new best friend. Available in a wide variety of colors, they are perfect for painting strong graphic images. Use the graphics in this book or check out logos, comic art, and poster art for design ideas.

My favorite way to use paint pens is for wall murals. I project the artwork onto the wall (see Enlarging Your Image on page 13), trace it with a paint pen, and then color in the drawing "coloring book" style using color washes (watered-down paint) and a soft paint brush. The process is simple and fast, and in no time at all you can make a blank wall look like a page from a storybook. A wealth of design inspiration can be found in coloring books, comic books, stencil designs, and rubber stamp designs.

Practice your artwork on paper, poster board, or canvas before graduating to more permanent surfaces such as doors and walls. Canvas makes a great painting medium for both large- and small-scale projects, and you can bring a canvas with you if you move.

Portability has other advantages as well. How will you be able to gain international fame as an artist without some portable masterpieces?

USING PAINT PENS

Once you have chosen and projected your design, you are ready to start painting. The paint pens I used in this book are Painters®. They are fast drying non-toxic acrylic paint markers and are very easy to use. Just shake and depress the nib of the pen until the paint flows, and use the pen in the same way you would a felt marker. Choose your nib size according to the detail of your painting. Use a fine tipped pen for fine detail and a broad tipped pen to fill in large areas. Sometimes you will need two coats of paint to get the coverage you want. Since the paint dries quickly, you don't have to wait long before applying a second coat. Remember to put the cap back on your pen when you are finished painting or the pen will dry out.

Before you start your painting project, change into clothes that are not your Sunday best just in case you get some paint on yourself. I don't follow my own advice and now all my clothes are "paint clothes"! It is also a good idea to protect the floor with newspaper or a drop cloth in case you drop a pen. This is especially good advice if you don't want your painting career cut short by parents unimpressed with paint splatters on the carpet.

NOTE TO PARENTS

Not all paint pens are the same. Make sure to chose a brand that is non-toxic certified and fast drying. Paint pen projects are ideal for both children and adults. However, since small children may not restrict their artwork to the project at hand, adult supervision is advised.

LET THE FUN BEGIN

Let's begin by walking step-by-step through a couple of projects. In the first project all the painting is done with paint pens. In the second project paint pens are used in partnership with color washes.

Once you have mastered these two exercises you will have the skills to do any of the paint pen projects in this book.

Get your paint pen pumped for action. You are ready to take off on a great painting adventure.

BASIC MATERIALS FOR ALL PROJECTS

- A line drawing or picture
- A method of enlarging your image (photocopier, light projector, or grid system)
- Pen or pencil and carbon or transfer paper if you don't use a projector
- Paint pens in sizes and colors as needed for project

- Water-based paints in a variety of colors for projects using color washes
- Artist's brushes for projects using color washes
- An acrylic sealer or topcoat to protect colorwashed painting

Note: Special tools and materials are listed for each project in the book. Those given above will be needed for all projects.

Butterfly

1. Trace over your projected or transferred drawing of the butterfly with a fine black paint pen.

Step 1

Step 2a   Step 2b   Step 3

2. Fill in the black sections with a black paint pen.

3. Fill in the colored sections of the butterfly using fine or medium tip paint pens in pink, pearlescent pink, and yellow. You may need to give the colored sections two coats of paint to get the coverage you want. Let the first coat dry before applying a second. The paint dries quickly but you can speed up the process with a hairdryer if you wish.

Teddy Bear

1. Using a medium tip brown paint pen trace over your projected or transferred image of the bear.

Step 1

2. Using an artist's watercolor brush color in the beige sections of the bear with a color wash. To make the color wash pour a little paint into the bottom of a glass, add some water, and mix. The ratio of paint to water will depend on the type of water-based paint you use so you will need to experiment. Try out your color wash on paper. If it is too intense, add more water. If it is too weak, add more paint. It is safer to add too little paint than too much, because if you want stronger color in your artwork you can always apply more coats once the first coat has dried.

Step 2

Step 3

3. Using a ¾″ flat artist's brush fill in the brown areas of the bear with a warm brown color wash.

4. If you wish to shade certain areas, apply more coats of the color wash until you have achieved the desired effect. Each time you add another coat of paint, the color deepens.

Step 4

Comic Relief

Are your parents giving you a hard time about cleaning your room? This damsel in distress should dispel any domestic unrest brewing over messy bedrooms. Ever notice how difficult it is to be angry when you're laughing? Maybe it should be mandatory for teenagers to post such warnings on their bedroom doors!

SPECIAL TOOLS AND MATERIALS

- Fine tip paint pen in black and red
- Medium tip paint pens in black, yellow, and blue
- Round artist's brush
- Flesh-toned water-based paint or craft acrylic paint

Guard Frog

IF YOUR STANDARDS for a tidy room differ greatly from your parents', here's another suggestion. Post this little tree frog on your door. He won't help you clean up your room, but he may give you more privacy. If that doesn't work, at least he's given your parents fair warning that a jungle could be lurking behind closed doors.

SPECIAL TOOLS AND MATERIALS

- Medium tip paint pen in black
- Fine tip paint pens in yellow, white, orange, black, green, light green, and pale orange
- Pen or pencil

Method

1 Use a photocopier to print out the artwork at the size you wish it to appear on your door.

2 If your door is not white, paint a section of it white. Use painter's tape to define this area for painting. Allow the white paint to dry for several days before painting with the paint pens.

3 Place the carbon paper or transfer paper under your photocopy, and tape them in place on the door.

4 Use a pen or pencil to trace over the photocopied design. Make sure you press hard enough to leave a good impression from the carbon or transfer paper.

5 Using paint pens, trace over and color in your design.

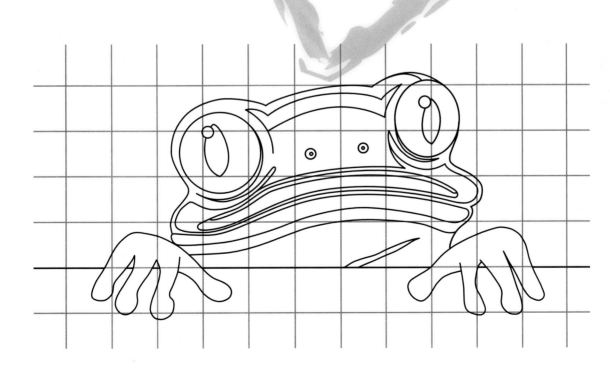

Butterfly World

Wᴴᴇɴ ɪ ᴡᴀꜱ in school, my passion for doodling earned me the label "apathy personified" from my Grade Twelve English teacher, Mr. Waite. Little did he or I know that my doodling was valuable training for painting this butterfly world that is really nothing more than a giant doodling project. But with this butterfly world, you need not restrict your palette to blue ink from a ballpoint pen. Pick any color in the rainbow, and experiment with special effects paint pens to give the project extra pizzazz.

SPECIAL TOOLS AND MATERIALS

- Fine tip black paint pen
- Medium tip paint pens in black, baby blue, orange, and pink
- Painters® Pearlescent paint pens in pink, blue, purple, burnt orange, and white

Method

1 Project and trace the black portions of your butterflies with black paint pens. If you don't have a projector, or if your butterflies are in an awkward spot for projecting, use a photocopier to enlarge the designs to the size you desire. To use a photocopy:

a) Place carbon or transfer paper under your photocopy and tape them in place where you wish the butterflies to appear on your wall.

b) Trace the designs with a pen or stylus to transfer them onto the wall.

c) Trace over the transferred design with a paint pen. Use a medium tip pen for the broader areas of the design and a fine tip pen for the details.

2 Choose from an array of colored paint pens and special effects pens (I used pearlescent paint pens) to bring your butterflies to life. It will probably take two coats of paint to get the desired coverage. Don't worry if you accidentally paint over your black lines. You can touch them up later by retracing with your black paint pen.

Dig This

THE **World Record**

ALL ROUND THE GLOBE — ABSOLUTELY FREE

APRIL 1, 2002

DINOSAUR BONES DISCOVERED BY CHILDREN

SIDNEY, BC *(Associated Press)* Dinosaur bones dating back to the Cretaceous Era were recently unearthed by two children playing in their back yard in the small town of Sidney on Vancouver Island. Jimmy and Jessica Smith, aged nine and eleven, were attempting to dig a hole to China in their mother's delphinium garden when they made an amazing discovery of a complete set of dinosaur bones. A local palaeontologist from the University of Victoria was unable to identify the species, and there is speculation that this type of dinosaur may become known as a Smithosaurus in recognition of the children who discovered it. The bones are on display and may be viewed in the children's bedroom.

SPECIAL TOOLS AND MATERIALS

- Wall paint
- White paint pens

Method

1 If your wall is white or off-white, you will need to paint the room another color so your dinosaur bones show up.

2 Project the design to the size you desire then trace the outline of the design with a paint pen. Once the design is traced, use a paint pen to fill it. Apply two coats of paint for good coverage.

NOTE: If your dinosaur is large, you will need at least two paint pens to complete your painting. Use a pen with a small nib for small projects and a pen with a larger nib for large projects.

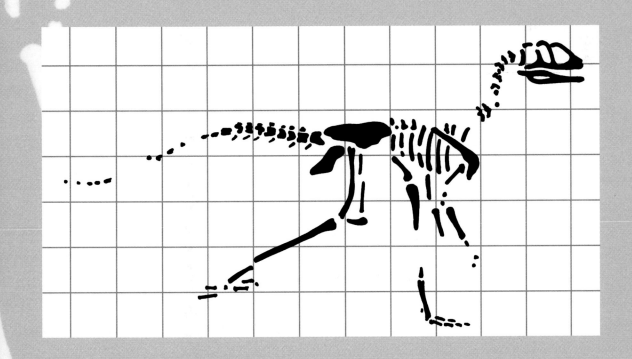

Best Laid Plans

"May I go out and play?" Harry asked.
"Not unless you take your sister," said his mother.
"Take my sister," whined Harry. "I don't want her tagging along."

Harry had big plans for the day. He had been secretly crafting a little river raft out of twigs and bits of string. Today was to be launch day and he pictured himself spending the afternoon basking in the sun as he captained his little vessel downstream. His sister didn't fit into any of his plans.

"You heard what I said," his mother insisted.

It was all Nancy, Harry's sister, could do to suppress her grin. She had plans too. Harry was in for a big surprise.

SPECIAL TOOLS AND MATERIALS

- Ultra fine black paint pen
- Color washes in blue, light blue, pale yellow, pink, and golden brown
- Round artist's brush
- Acrylic clearcoat

Method

1 Use a photocopier to enlarge the pattern to the desired size.

2 Place carbon or transfer paper under your photocopy, and tape it in place where you wish the image to appear on the object you are painting.

3 Trace the drawing with a pen or stylus to transfer the image onto your painting surface.

4 Trace over the transferred design with an ultra fine paint pen.

5 Use color washes and artist's brushes to color in your paint pen drawing.

6 Seal with an acrylic clearcoat. Color washes don't have the same durability as undiluted paints, so a clearcoat seals and protects the artwork.

Furious

YOU MIGHT WONDER why a young man would have a cartoon painted on his garbage bin. Well, it is not just any cartoon, it is Furious, and he is the logo and mascot for my son Kirk's ultimate team. This courageous chimp has helped inspire the team to win five national championships and two world titles in recent years, pushing Canada to number one on the world stage.

Use this logo or your own team logo to paint an array of objects. You can even use paint pens on T-shirts, bedding, and curtains. To prevent fabric from wiggling while you paint it, place it over a piece of non-corrugated cardboard that has been sprayed with stencil adhesive. When painting on fabric, "heat set" your artwork once the paint is dry. To do this, place an ironing cloth over the painting and then iron at a high setting. Wait at least ten days before washing the fabric, and wash it in cold water. Practice on a piece of scrap fabric first.

Caution: Get an adult to help you with spraying stencil adhesive and using a hot iron.

SPECIAL TOOLS AND MATERIALS

- Paint pens in yellow and white
- Spray enamel (for basecoating before painting with paint pens on metal)

Method

1 Use a photocopier to enlarge or reduce the logo to the desired size.

2 Transfer the design onto your object to be painted by placing carbon paper or transfer paper under your photocopy before taping it in place.

3 Use a pen or pencil to trace over your photocopied design. Make sure you press hard enough to leave a clear impression from the carbon or transfer paper.

4 Using paint pens, trace over and fill in your design. Use medium, fine, or ultra fine tipped pens depending on the size of your logo.

Easy Rider

W ALL ART doesn't get any cooler than this life-size classic motorcycle. Poised to transport you anywhere your imagination can carry you, this motorcycle's appeal reaches free-spirited people of all ages.

I painted this mural for a friend of mine who is reveling in his second childhood (name withheld by request). It portrays the spirit of "Born to be Wild," the theme song of the movie *Easy Rider:*

Head out on the highway
Looking for adventure
And whatever comes our way

Ride on, Don . . . Oops!

NOTE TO PARENTS: Don't worry, it's only paint.

SPECIAL TOOLS AND MATERIALS

- Black paint pens – one fine, one medium, and two large tip
- Acrylic clearcoat
- High density foam roller

Method

1 Project the drawing of the motorcycle onto your wall and trace all around the outside of the vehicle and the black sections. Use a fine tip paint pen in areas where there is fine detail. If you have any younger brothers or sisters, don't let them in your room at this stage because it is important that the projector not be jiggled while you are doing this tracing. Put on your favorite music and sing along so your siblings know you are having a really good time. Before long their fingers will be itching to try out the paint pens.

2 Use black paint pens to fill in the black sections of the design. Choose the size of the pen according to the detail of the area you are coloring. It will take a while for you to color in all these sections, and you may welcome a little help. If you have played your cards right, and if you have a sibling old enough, help will be close at hand.

3 Protect your artwork by applying an acrylic clearcoat. I used a matte acrylic finish by Liquitex and applied it with a high density foam roller.

Hanging Out

W HEN I LOOK at this baby orangutan, I smile, remembering my nephew as a small boy. Just like this baby, Daniel was as cute as a button, and full of mischief. He literally used to climb the walls, and his favorite place to hang out was on door casings. Now that he has grown into a young man, he still prefers to be off the ground. He is a pilot!

If you are too timid to paint a full-scale mural on your bedroom wall, start by personalizing the entrance to your room with original artwork. You could paint this artwork on a canvas to be mounted on your door or you could paint it directly on the door. Door projects, which are small in scope, can be changed often. This means that great bunny you painted on your door when you were six needn't still be there when you are sixteen.

SPECIAL TOOLS AND MATERIALS

- Medium or fine tip paint pens in brown, black, and green
- Artist's brush
- Color washes in flesh color, terra-cotta, and spring green
- Matte or satin acrylic clearcoat

Method

1 Project the line drawing for the orangutan, positioning the design where you wish the painted image to appear.

2 Trace the eyes using a black paint pen.

3 Trace the rest of the orangutan with a brown paint pen, and trace the vines with a dark green pen.

4 Use a flesh-toned color wash (acrylic paint diluted with water) with an artist's brush to paint the little guy's hands and feet, and around his eyes and mouth.

5 In a similar fashion, use a terra-cotta color wash to paint the rest of his body and a spring green color wash to fill in the vines. You need not be overly careful when painting with the color washes, because they are very thin and will not show up if they are accidentally applied over areas done with a paint pen.

6 Protect your completed artwork by applying an acrylic clearcoat following the manufacturer's instructions.

Mermaid

Beautiful scales, under sparkling sun,
Effortless swimmer, do you wish you were one?
But better yet – come play with me,
Under the water, in the sea.
No, better yet –
I'll meet you halfway,
I'll come to your house –
What do you say?

Who could turn down an invitation like
that? If bath time wasn't fun before, it
will be now!

SPECIAL TOOLS AND MATERIALS

- Medium tip brown paint pen
- Color washes
- Matte or satin acrylic clearcoat
- ¾" flat artist's brush (goat hair or hake)
- Medium sized round artist's brush

Method

1 If your wall is not white, paint a section of it white. Use painter's tape to define this area for painting. Allow the white paint to dry for several days before painting with paint pens and color washes.

2 Project the line drawing onto the wall and trace the drawing with the brown paint pen.

3 Color in the line drawing with the color washes, using a ¾" flat artist's brush for the large areas and a medium sized round artist's brush for the smaller areas. Test out your color washes on paper before painting the wall to make sure the colors are not too strong. It is better to use paint that is too weak rather than too strong because you can always add another coat of paint when the first dries to intensify the color.

4 Protect your finished artwork with an acrylic clearcoat.

Teddy Bears' Picnic

AT LUNCHTIME, when I was a little girl, my mother would set up a tiny fold-down table for my brother, sister, and me. She would serve us soft-boiled eggs with bread and butter cut into fingers that she stacked like a log cabin, and we'd listen to a children's radio show that always played "The Teddy Bears' Picnic."

> *If you go down to the woods today*
> *You're sure of a big surprise*
> *If you go down to the woods today*
> *You'd better go in disguise*
> *For every bear there ever was*
> *Will gather there for certain, because*
> *Today's the day the teddy bears have their picnic.*

We would sing along (off key, of course) and I remember wondering how it was possible for people to be so tiny they could fit into our radio. I did say I was *very* young, didn't I?

SPECIAL TOOLS AND MATERIALS

- Medium tip brown paint pen
- Color washes
- Matte or satin acrylic clearcoat
- ¾" flat artist's brush (goat hair or hake)
- High density foam roller

Method

1 Project the line drawing **1** onto the wall and trace the tree, hill, and grass with a medium tip brown paint pen.

2 Project and position line drawing **2** under the tree and similarly trace the bears, the honey pot, and the blanket

3 Color in the line drawing using color washes and a ¾" flat artist's brush.

4 It is better to make your color washes too weak, rather than too strong. You can always add more layers of the wash if you wish to intensify the color.

5 Protect your finished artwork with an acrylic clearcoat. I used a matte finish and applied it with a high density foam roller.

HONEY

Pleasantville Playmat

I WORKED ON the planning stages for this playmat when my friend, Lynda, and her eight-year-old son, Ian, visited from England. Together we became town planners striving to create the perfect village. Essentials such as playgrounds and candy stores were easily agreed upon. But when it came time to test our road system, there was trouble in Paradise. Ian, being English, drove his little cars on the left side of the road. I, a Canadian, insisted on driving on the right side. It became all too apparent that two more essential services were needed – a tow truck and a collision repair shop.

SPECIAL TOOLS AND MATERIALS

- 40" × 60" piece of vinyl flooring
- White acrylic primer
- White eggshell or low luster paint
- Paint brushes or rollers for applying the primer, basecoat, and topcoat
- Pencil
- Fine tip black paint pen
- Fine tip white paint pen
- Carbon or transfer paper
- Painter's tape
- Gray paint
- Yardstick
- Fine tip paint pens in black, white, and taupe
- Medium tip paint pens in blue, red, orange, and baby blue
- Yellow-green, green, and brown color washes
- Artists's brushes for applying the color washes
- Water-based clear topcoat (matte or satin finish)
- Stencil roller

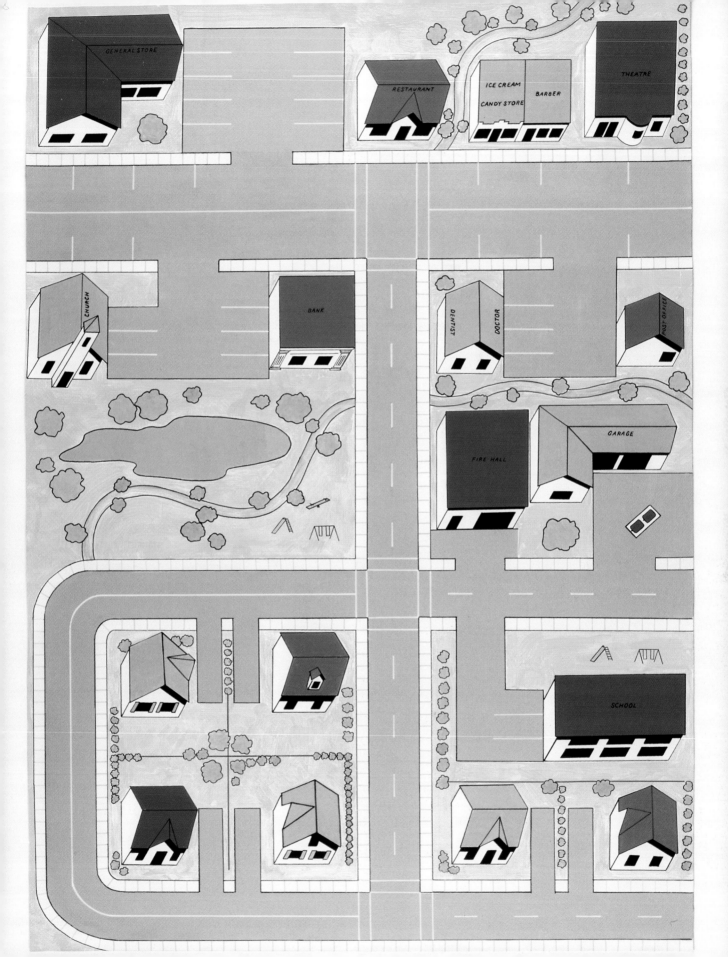

Method

1 Paint the underside of the flooring with a high quality acrylic primer and let dry before basecoating with a low luster white paint. Your painting will be done over this basecoat once it is well dried.

2 Use the grid system (see page 14) to enlarge the pattern so it fits the mat. Draw the layout in pencil. You may wish to enlarge the drawings of the buildings using a photocopier and then transfer these images onto the mat using carbon or transfer paper.

3 Stencil the roads gray using painter's tape to act as a stencil to define the roadways. (See instructions for stenciling on page 66.)

4 Use a yardstick and white fine tip paint pen to paint the road markings.

5 Using a taupe pen draw in the sidewalk squares.

6 Trace the outlines for the buildings, walkways, trees, play equipment, and gas pumps using a fine tip black paint pen.

7 Use color washes to paint the lawns, walkways, and shrubs.

8 Color the rooftops and pond with paint pens.

9 Label the buildings with a fine tip black paint pen.

10 Topcoat the playmat with a water based varnish.

11 Get out your Hot Wheels and bring the town to life.

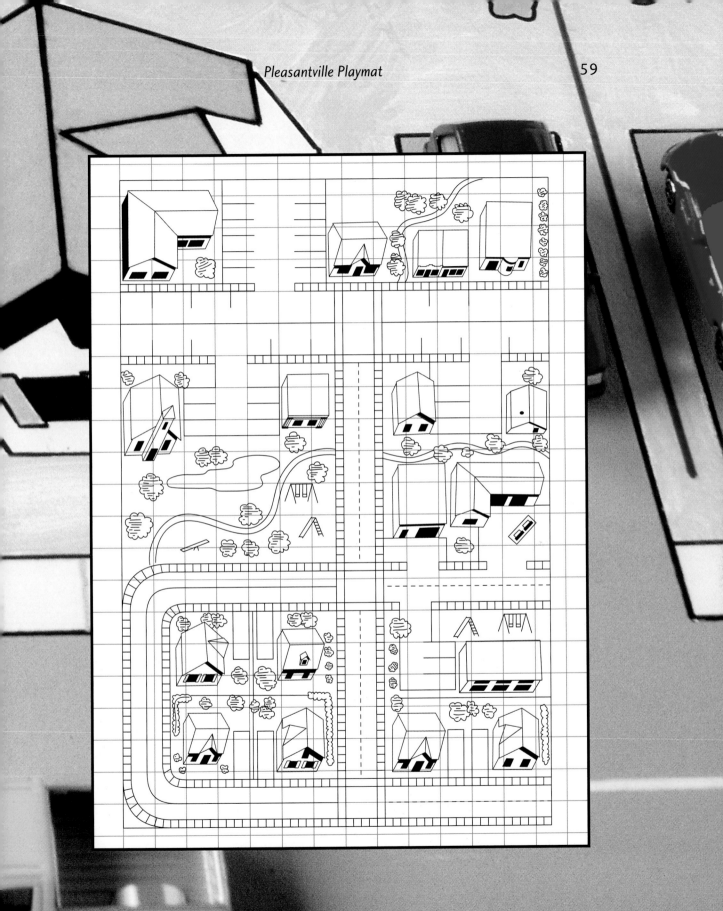

Projection Stenciling

PROJECTION STENCILING is a technique that lets you take almost any image and turn it into a stencil of any size. With just a beginner's knowledge of stenciling, you can create your own custom artwork from almost any printed picture, including illustrations from children's storybooks, art books, and comic books, pictures in magazines, clip art, favorite photos, and more.

Projection stenciling involves selecting a picture to copy into a giant stencil and then cutting out and stenciling the picture one color at a time. Think of projection stenciling as big paint-by-numbers projects.

Before you dive into a projection stenciling project, you need to learn the basics of stenciling. Then take a few minutes to read about the steps leading up to stenciling your enlarged artwork.

These include enlarging your image, tracing it onto freezer paper, and cutting out sections of the design for stenciling. Once you master these simple steps, you are ready to take on just about any art project. No more stick men for you!

BASICS OF STENCILING

What Is a Stencil?

A stencil is a thin piece of material with a design cut out of it. Plastic, metal, cardboard, and paper are all popular stencil materials. We use freezer paper for the projects in this book because it is inexpensive and cuts easily.

What is Stenciling?

Stenciling is the art of applying paint through the openings in a stencil to print out a painted copy of the stencil design.

WHAT MATERIALS DO I NEED?

Stencil Material

All the stencil projects in this book were done with freezer paper. Freezer paper is a brown or white paper coated on one side with a thin film of plastic. It is easy to cut, comes in large rolls, and is readily available at almost any supermarket or butcher shop. If you can't find it there, it is available online at www.buckinghamstencils.com.

Paint

You can use almost any water-based paint for stenciling as long as it isn't too watery. Search through your house and see what you can turn up. Household latex paints work well, as do craft acrylic paints and roller stencil paint. Don't use oil-based paints because they take too long to dry. Also, cleanup for oil-based paints requires using solvents and parents will prefer projects that can be cleaned up with soap and water.

Blending Glaze

Some paints, such as craft acrylic paint, dry so fast that they build up on your stencil brush or rollers. If you add about 20% blending glaze to craft acrylic paint you can slow down the drying time of the paint, and less paint will build up on your paint applicator. You can also use blending glaze to make paint more translucent. For the colored glazes used in this book we mixed one part acrylic paint with three or four parts glaze.

Stencil Adhesive

This is low tack (not very sticky) glue that you spray on the back (non-shiny side) of your freezer paper so that the paper lies nicely against the wall. Spray the paper outside or in a well-ventilated room and allow the stencil adhesive to dry for a few minutes before placing the paper on the wall. If you find your wall is still a bit sticky after you remove your freezer paper, let the stenciling dry for a few days, then have an adult moisten a clean rag with paint thinner and very lightly rub the wall surface. This will remove any lingering tackiness from the spray adhesive.

Caution: Remember to check the safety precautions and instructions on the spray glue before using. Young children should never use spray glue, and adult supervision is recommended for older children.

Stencil Brushes

Use a good quality stencil brush that has soft, supple, densely packed bristles. Stencil brushes come in a variety of sizes, usually ranging from ¼" to 1". Use large brushes to stencil large openings, and small brushes for more detailed painting. You need a clean, dry brush for each color of paint. These are available at craft and art supply stores or online at www.buckinghamstencils.com.

Stencil Rollers

Stencil rollers are high density foam rollers with rounded heads. They are made just for stenciling and can be found at art and craft supply stores and online at www.buckinghamstencils.com. Don't use soft foam rollers or nap rollers for stenciling, as they hold too much paint and won't give you a clean-edged print. You need a clean, dry roller for each color of paint.

Palette

A palette is simply a tray on which you can pour your paint. You can use a styrofoam tray, a cookie sheet, or a paint palette that you buy in a store.

Spreading Tool

For roller stenciling you need a broad spatula or Popsicle stick for spreading a thin layer of paint on your palette.

Paper Towels

These are handy for removing excess paint from your brush or roller. They come in handy for wiping up spills too, but of course there won't be any!

Black Permanent Felt Marker

Use a black permanent fine tip felt marker to trace your pattern onto the freezer paper.

Painter's or Low-tack Tape

Use this to help support the weight of the stencil paper once it is on the wall.

Utility Knives or X-ACTO Knives

These knives are used to cut the stencil designs in the freezer paper. I like to use utility knives with snap-off blades with a sharp angle, similar to X-ACTO blades. It is really important to replace your blade often so you are always cutting with a sharp blade. With utility knives, a fresh blade is just a snap away.

Caution: X-ACTO blades and utility knives are razor-sharp and should never be used by young children. Use extreme care with these knives. Replace the cap on an X-ACTO knife after use. If you are using a utility knife be sure to retract its blade and lock it in safety position when you are finished working.

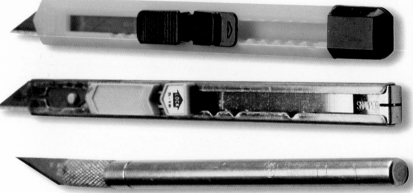

GETTING STARTED

This little exercise will teach you the basics of stenciling. I know, I know, it doesn't look very exciting, but once you master this you can do any projection stenciling project in the book. Think of it this way – eat your vegetables and then you can have dessert.

1. Cut out two 10″ squares of freezer paper to use as your stencil material.

2. Draw or trace a circle on the shiny side of each piece of paper using a permanent felt tip pen.

3. Place the freezer paper on a cutting board or piece of non-corrugated cardboard and use an X-ACTO knife or utility knife to cut along the outlines of the circles. Remove the cutouts.

4. Place the stencils shiny side down and spray them with stencil adhesive.

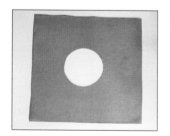

5. Lay the stencils shiny side up on a piece of paper and press into place. Use one stencil to practice roller stenciling and the other to practice brush stenciling. You will need to learn both techniques to do the projects in this book. Roller stenciling is great for filling in large areas with even paint coverage, whereas brush stenciling is more appropriate for stenciling small openings and adding detail.

ROLLER STENCILING

1. Pour a small amount of red paint onto your palette.

2. Use your spreader to draw out a long, thin film of paint.

3. Run a clean, dry stencil roller through the full length of the drawn-out paint.

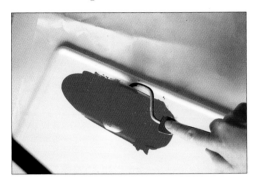

4. Roll your roller back and forth vigorously several times to load the paint evenly.

5. Remove excess paint from your roller by rolling it back and forth several times on paper towels. You will be surprised at how little paint you need. Stenciling, whether with a brush or a roller, is almost a "no

paint" technique. If you run the roller over your hand you should see very little paint.

6. Run the roller back and forth across the whole stencil, pressing lightly at first. Build up the paint gradually for more color depth.

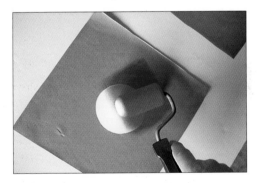

Hint: Prevent your roller from drying out when you take a break by putting it into a small Ziploc bag.

BRUSH STENCILING

1. Pour a small amount of red paint onto your palette.

2. Dip a clean, dry stencil brush into your paint. Using a circular motion, work the paint well into your brush.

3. Remove most of the paint on a paper

towel using a circular motion. Your brush should feel almost dry.

4. Hold the brush straight up and down and use either a circular motion or an up-and-down stippling motion to apply the paint.

Hint: When you are doing larger projects you may find that your brush is developing a buildup of paint or is drying out. You can solve this problem by swiping your brush across a moist sponge or by working blending glaze into the bristles. Whichever method you use, make sure to dry your brush on a paper towel before you go back to stenciling.

To add dimension to your stenciling use a stencil brush to shade and highlight.

SHADING

Load your stenciling brush with dark red paint and then unload most of the paint onto a paper towel. Position the brush so it is partially on the stencil and partially on the surface you are painting. Use a circular motion to follow around the outside edge of the cutout. This will result in color that is strongest at the outer edge and becomes fainter as it moves toward the center of your ball (Step 1). If you remove the stencil paper at this point your ball will look like this (Step 2).

HIGHLIGHTING

Use white paint to add highlights to your ball. Work the white paint into your brush and then offload most of the paint onto a paper towel. Rub the brush in a circular fashion wherever you wish to create a highlight (Step 3). Remove the stencil paper (Step 4).

Now that you have your ball painted, you are ready to roll!

Before moving on to bigger and better projects (for example, the giraffe) we need to have a word about cutting instructions.

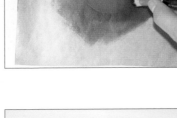

Step 1

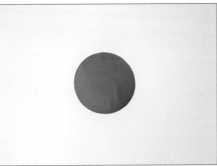

Step 2

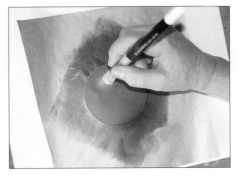

Step 3

Step 4

CUTTING INSTRUCTIONS

1. Use an X-ACTO knife or a utility knife to cut out your stencil. If you use an X-ACTO knife make sure to replace your blade often so that it cuts clean. Before cutting out your pattern make sure your freezer paper is positioned correctly so your painted image will appear where you want it.

2. Cut out your stencil directly on the surface you wish your painting to appear. Use a light touch with the knife in order not to score the wall (or other surface) too deeply. Some scoring is not a problem as when it comes time to repaint, a light sanding will make shallow score lines disappear. If you wish to avoid any scoring, use a finger to lift the freezer paper slightly off the surface as you cut along the pattern lines. *Caution:* Utility or X-ACTO knives should never be used by young children, and older children should always be helped by an adult to cut out stencils.

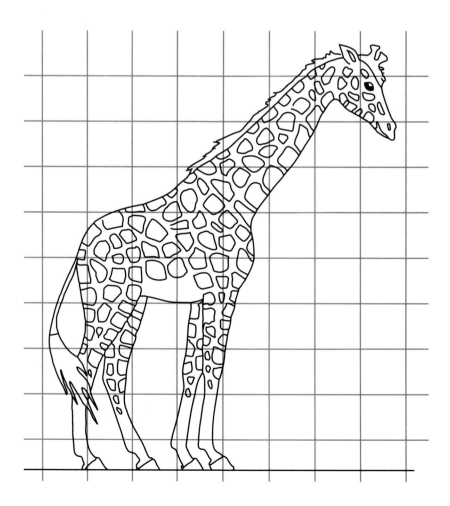

Giraffe

Using our giraffe image, follow the steps of projection stenciling to take this image from a printed page to a painting on a wall.

1. Follow the instructions in Enlarging Your Image (page 13-14).

2. Project your drawing and trace it onto freezer paper as described in Tracing Your Image (page 15).

3. Cut out around the outside of the giraffe's body and remove this large cutout.

4. Roller stencil the cutout area light golden tan. It may take several coats of paint to build up good paint coverage. Be careful to use the dry stenciling technique around the cut edges of the stencil. You don't want any paint to seep under the paper.

5. Use a large stencil brush and the dry stenciling technique to shade around the outside of the giraffe with a deeper tan.

6. Replace the cutout. Cut out the giraffe's horns, mane, eye, hooves, and tip of the tail.

7. Stencil these cutout areas brown.

8. Replace the cutout for the mane and cut out the giraffe's spots.

9. Stencil these openings terra-cotta.

10. Remove the freezer paper. Ta-da!

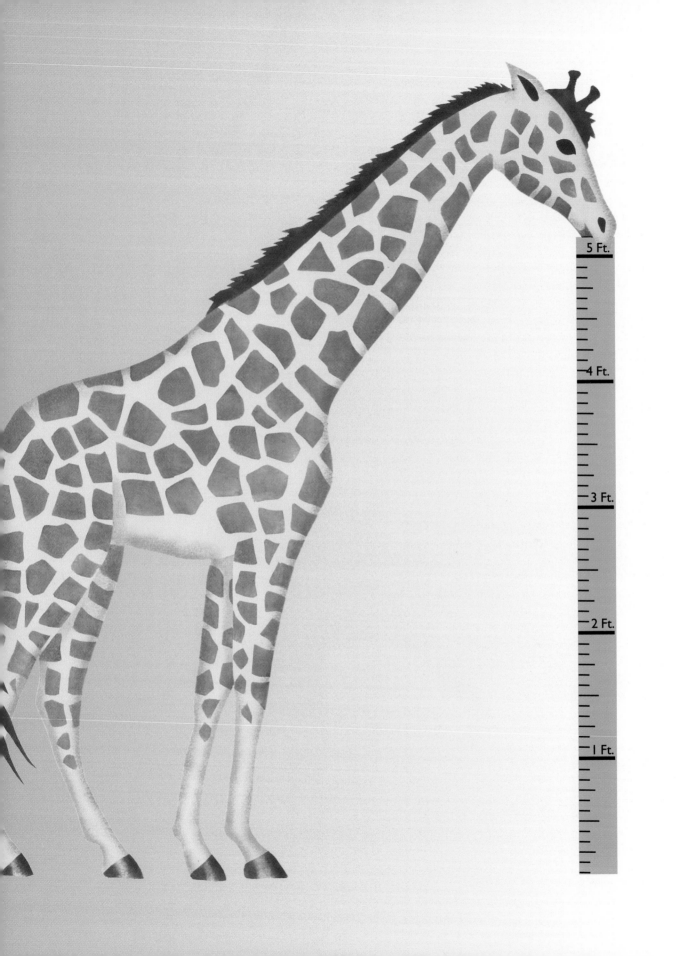

5 Ft.

4 Ft.

3 Ft.

2 Ft.

1 Ft.

Little Projects, Big Ideas

WHEN YOU ANNOUNCE to your parents that you are going to paint artwork on your bedroom wall, your announcement is greeted with much enthusiasm. No? Well, maybe you should start with a small project first to get your family on your side. Parents, like pets, need conditioning from time to time to keep them on track (your track, of course). Once you have gained their confidence with small projects, you are well on your way to bigger and better endeavors!

Start with ladybugs first. Everyone loves these. You can do your tarantulas later.

SPECIAL TOOLS AND MATERIALS

- Red, white, and black paint
- Stencil brushes
- Stencil roller (optional)
- Pencil

Method

1 Paint the surface white and let this basecoat dry overnight.

2 Position your freezer paper pattern in place and cut out all around the outside of the ladybugs' bodies. Leave this cutout in place.

3 Cut along the outline of the bugs' red wings and remove these cutouts, saving them for replacement later.

4 Use a stencil roller or a large stencil brush to stencil the wings red and highlight them by either shading or highlighting (see Shading and Highlighting in the Basics of Stenciling, page 69).

5 For shading, use a stencil brush to build up strong color in some areas and allow the original white to show through as a highlight in others. Alternatively, you can highlight by stenciling white paint over the red paint where you wish the highlight to appear.

6 Replace the wing cutouts, and cut out and remove all the black bits (legs, antennae, head, and spots). Stencil these openings black. Make sure the eyes are still covered with freezer paper so they stay white.

7 Remove the freezer paper. Use a pencil to draw a line separating the bugs' white eyes from the background white (see photo).

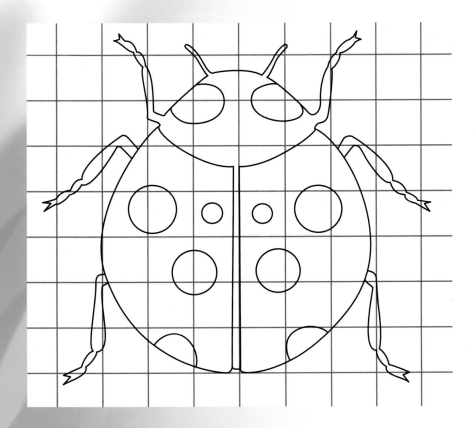

Lasting Impression

THE VANCOUVER GRIZZLES' number one fan, Toby King, was heartbroken when the Grizzlies packed up and left Vancouver for Memphis, but Toby's mom and I came to the rescue. We painted an almost life-sized Grizzlie on his bedroom wall. The Grizzlies may have left town, but they still have a huge presence in Toby's room.

If you are a sports fan, there is a vast range of sports from which to choose your action figures – hockey, baseball, soccer, rock climbing, skateboarding, surfing, weight lifting, gymnastics – the list is endless. Pictures from magazines, books, and posters are great, but even better would be pictures of your own team in action.

To Parents: Your child may be too young to paint his own mural, but he can get very involved in the planning stages. Toby went through all his basketball magazines and put Post-it notes on the pictures of players that he liked, and Georgina and I chose one of these to create our silhouette. Because Toby picked out the player for us to paint, we were pretty sure he would like our painting, and we weren't disappointed. We took "Ooooooh! Wow! Awesome!" as a pretty clear endorsement.

SPECIAL TOOLS AND MATERIALS

- Stencil roller
- Latex paint several shades darker than your wall color

Method

1 Make sure you spray your freezer paper well before affixing it to the wall, because there are many little pieces of freezer paper in the basketball net that need to stay on the wall while you stencil the net.

2 Cut along the outline of the basketball player and the net, and remove the cutouts.

3 Roller stencil the cutout areas. Make sure to use a dry roller technique near the cut edges of the paper. It will take several coats of paint to build up good coverage, so you may wish to speed up the drying time between coats with a hairdryer.

4 Remove the freezer paper. Wow!

Larger Than Life

Yᴏᴜ ᴍᴀʏ ʙᴇ a teenager living at home, but that doesn't mean your decor needs to reflect your dependent status. This larger-than-life guitar would be equally at home in a Manhattan townhouse, a bohemian loft, or your bedroom. Boxcar-red paint spills from one wall, mustard-colored paint from another, and together they paint a strong graphic that could be uptown, downtown, or anywhere in between. Just make sure your parents don't become so fond of your artwork that they start hanging out in your room.

SPECIAL TOOLS AND MATERIALS

- Mustard, boxcar red, vibrant blue, light yellow, and white paint
- Four stencil rollers (or one roller and three refills)
- Painter's tape
- Stylus or similar sharp instrument
- Ruler

Method

1 Basecoat the wall boxcar red, and allow adequate drying time before positioning the freezer paper and tracing the projected pattern.

2 Cut out as one piece the mustard and yellow bar under the guitar's strings. Save this piece. Stencil the opening light yellow. Once the paint dries, replace this cutout.

3 Cut out all the mustard colored sections of the design and roller stencil them mustard.

4 Cut out the blue opening in the guitar and stencil it vibrant blue.

5 Before removing the freezer paper from the wall, mark the placement for the guitar strings by poking a hole with a sharp instrument (stylus) through the paper, indenting pinprick markings on the wall to show the placements for the strings.

6 Use painter's tape to define the strings to be stenciled, allowing a ¼" gap between lengths of tape for the strings. Stencil the strings white.

Standing Tall

A LARGE GIRAFFE painted on a bedroom wall will cer-
tainly attract attention, but you want to make sure it
is the right kind of attention. Standing alone in the room
it will look like a fish out of water. Short of painting the
whole room to resemble an African savanna, you need
some way to make the giraffe feel at home. Here I have
paired a nuzzling mama giraffe and her baby. Together
they form a great frame over a bed.

NOTE TO PARENTS: Here's another way to handle the
"fish out of water." By partnering the mama giraffe with a
measuring stick you can create an innovative growth chart.
If you paint your growth chart on a piece of canvas rather
than on the wall, it becomes a moveable work of art and a
wonderful keepsake that can follow you should you move.

SPECIAL TOOLS AND MATERIALS

- Two stencil rollers (or one roller and one refill)
- One ¾" stencil brush
- One ½" stencil brush
- Light golden tan, tan, terra-cotta, and brown paint
- Paint pen (growth chart only)
- Painter's tape (growth chart only)
- Ruler (growth chart only)

Method

Mama and Baby

1. Cut out around the outside of the giraffes' bodies and roller stencil the cutout areas light golden tan.

2. Using a large stencil brush shade around the outside of the giraffes with a deeper tan.

3. Replace the cutouts.

4. Cut along the lines separating the giraffes' legs and the lines separating legs from the main bodies. Use these cut lines as guides to add shading. Lift the freezer paper along one side of the cut line (the side on which you wish the shading to appear) and leave the other side in place. With a dry brush stenciling technique shade by rubbing tan paint in a linear fashion along the cut edge. (This type of stenciling is called *linear shading.*) Check the photograph for placement of the shading.

5. Cut out the giraffes' horns, manes, eyes, hooves, and tips of tails and stencil these areas brown.

6. Replace the cutouts for the manes.

7. Cut out the giraffes' spots and roller stencil these openings terra-cotta.

8. Remove all the freezer paper.

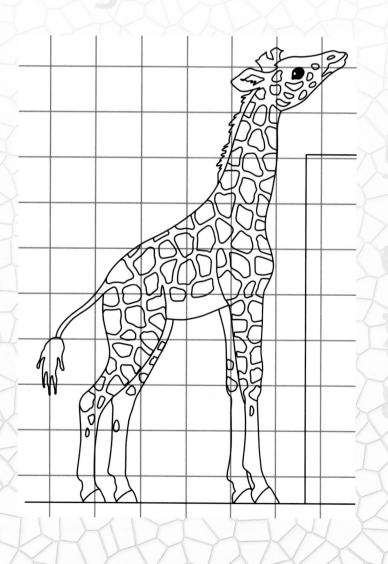

Growth Chart

Follow the instructions above for painting
the giraffe. Paint the measuring stick by using painter's tape to guide your stenciling,
and a paint pen to mark the measurements.

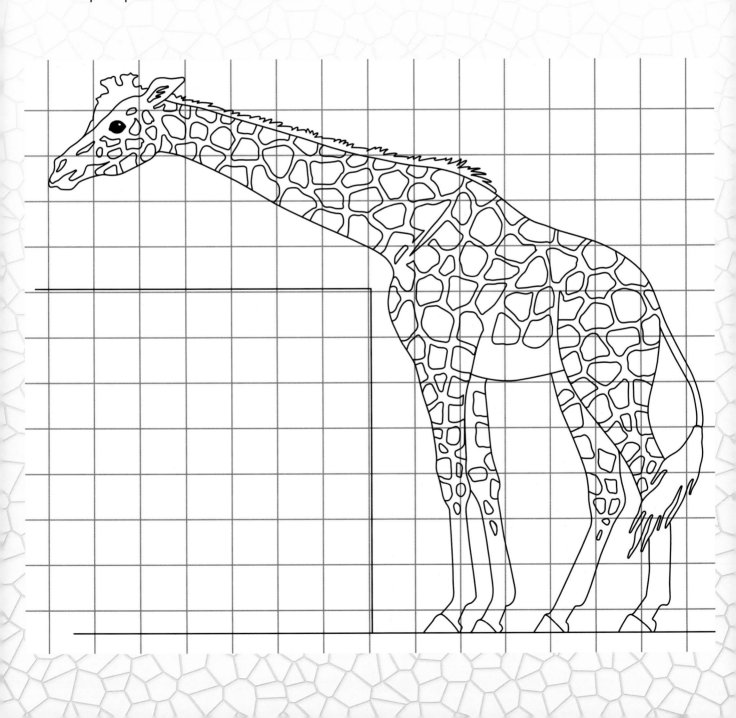

Just Ducky

Many families have a family pet such as a cat or dog, but in our family it's a rubber ducky who has faithfully followed us from house to house over the years. In recognition of his loyalty, I wanted to paint a larger-than-life portrait of Ducky over our bathtub. To paint the portrait I needed a snapshot of him in action. Unable to get the angle right for my shot in our small bathroom, I took Ducky with us on our summer vacation (yes, he's a real trooper!) and photographed him from my kayak. I paddled around him snapping pictures from this angle and that. Summer boaters, who threw curious glances in our direction, surrounded us. They looked at me, looked at Ducky, looked at each other, and exchanged comments. I am sure "What a quack!" was among them and I don't think they were talking about Ducky!

SPECIAL TOOLS AND MATERIALS

- Very pale yellow, pastel yellow, yellow, light green, black, pastel orange, and very pale orange paint
- Paint tinted lighter than the wall color
- Two stencil rollers (or one roller and one refill)
- Shadow glaze (one part raw umber paint, three parts water-based glaze)
- Stencil brushes in assorted sizes

Method

1 Cut out around the outside of the duck's entire body and remove this cutout.

2 Roller stencil this area pastel yellow.

3 With a stencil brush, shade around the outside of the ducky with a darker yellow, omitting the beak area. With the same stencil brush, shade the ducky's neck (see photo).

4 Use a large stencil brush and a very dry stenciling technique with pale yellow paint (pastel yellow mixed with white) to highlight the duck's head, chest, and inside of tail (see photo). Replace the cutout.

5 Cut out around the wing, cutting outside the shaded area and removing the wing cutout as one piece. With a small stencil brush and pale yellow paint, highlight along the top and right edge of the wing.

6 Replace the wing cutout.

7 Cut out the shadow area for the wing (see arrow) and for the feather tuft on the duck's head. Roller stencil these areas with shadow glaze.

8 Cut out the eye and stencil it black.

9 Cut out around the outside of the beak and stencil the beak pastel orange.

10 Use a stencil brush to highlight along the top of the beak with a paler orange and shade underneath the beak with shadow glaze. Once the paint dries, replace the beak cutout.

11 Cut out the inside of his mouth and stencil it with shadow glaze. Replace this cutout once the glaze dries.

12 Cut along the line separating the upper and lower sections of the beak. Flip the stencil paper to shade above this line with shadow glaze and highlight beneath it with very pale orange.

13 Cut along the line defining the ridge on the upper beak. Shade above this line with shadow glaze and highlight beneath it using very pale orange.

14 Cut out the ripples in the water and stencil them with paint tinted lighter than the wall. Remove the freezer paper.

Pandamonium

Tʜɪꜱ ᴘʟᴀʏꜰᴜʟ ᴍᴜʀᴀʟ was painted in the reading corner of a preschool by Marian Robinson and her fifteen-year-old daughter, Erin. Because the mural is so low to the ground Marian and Erin spent much of their time working on their knees. After several hours of such work Marian's knees began to ache. Erin had the perfect solution. The nursery school shared a building with a gymnastics school and Erin nipped next door to borrow a gym mat. There's more than one reason children should be involved in stenciling projects!

Note to Parents: This mural is great for introducing young children to the ABCs and colors.

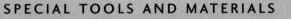

SPECIAL TOOLS AND MATERIALS

- Black, green, orange, purple, blue, yellow, white, and pink paint
- Seven stencil rollers (or one roller and six refills)
- Two large stencil brushes

Method

1 Cut out the letters and roller stencil them in bright colors, removing their cutouts and replacing them as necessary to paint adjacent letters.

2 Replace the "W" and "O" cutouts.

3 Cut out around the outside of the bears and remove these large cutouts. Make sure the little piece of freezer paper between the front legs of the upright bear stays stuck to the wall. Remove the cutouts, and add gray shading along the cut edge of the freezer paper. Refer to the photo for where to put the shading. Replace the cutouts.

Cut out the "W" bear's muzzle and leave this cutout in place. Remove the freezer paper surrounding the cutout to shade gray around the muzzle and then replace the paper.

5 Cut out the black sections of the bears and roller stencil them black.

6 Using a large stencil brush and a very dry stenciling technique, add white highlights to the black sections of the bears. See photo for placement of the highlights. The highlights will appear gray in colour, even though they were stenciled with white paint.

7 Replace the black cutouts with the exception of the mouths, noses, ears, and the leg of the little bear.

8 Cut along the lines where black meets black and refer to the photo for placing white highlights along these lines.

9 Cut along the lines where the white from one bear meets the white from the other and stencil gray along this edge. Refer to the photo for the placement of this shading.

10 Cut out the bears' eyes including the pupil. Stencil the eyes warm brown and replace the cutout when the paint dries. Cut out the pupils and stencil them black. Use the end of a small stencil brush dipped in white paint to dab a glint in the eyes.

11 Remove all the white cutouts and add extra shading to define neck, chin, and other areas. Refer to the photo for the placement of shading. Remove all freezer paper.

ABCDEFG

OPQRST

HIJKLMN

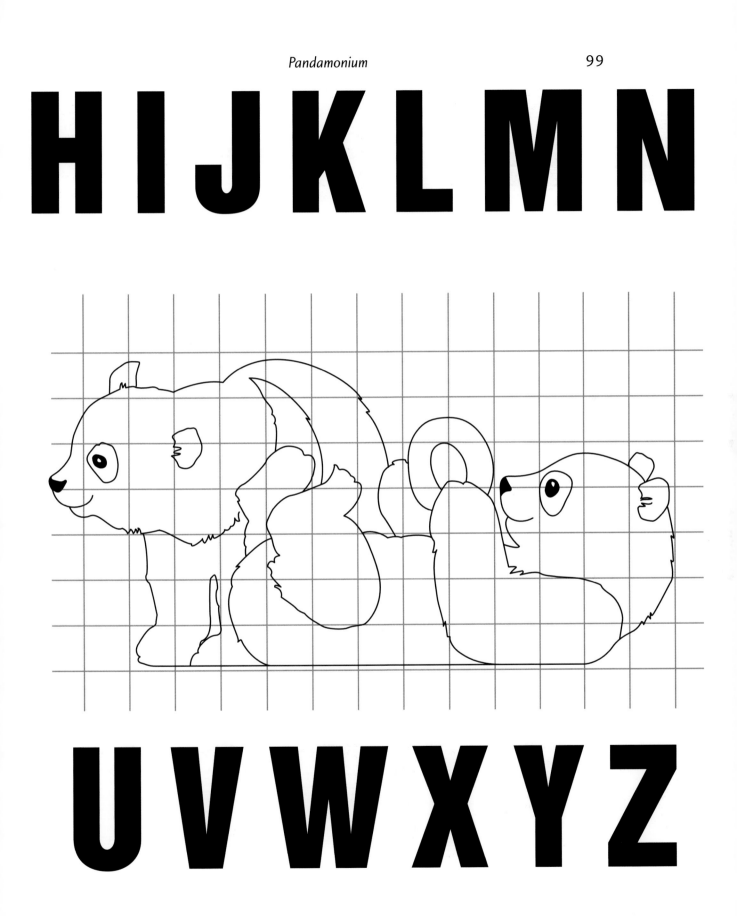

UVWXYZ

Flying Pigs

"WHO SAYS PIGS can't fly?" Pinky Pig shouted to his brother Walter. His heart was in his throat and he had never felt happier.

"Me," Walter replied in a small voice. His heart was in his throat too but he wouldn't be happy until he was back on the ground.

SPECIAL TOOLS AND MATERIAL

- Stencil brushes in assorted sizes
- Six stencil rollers (or one stencil roller and five refills)
- Paint in the following colors: white, light blue, pink fleshtone, pink, deep pink, brown, light brown, green, blue, yellow
- Medium tip gray paint pen
- Yardstick

Method

1 Cut out around the outside of the parachutes, cutting through the parachutes' lines in the process.

2 Roller stencil the openings white. When the paint dries, use a stencil brush and light blue paint to shade around the outside edge of the parachutes where the white of the parachute meets the sky. Replace the cutouts.

3 Cut out the undersides of the parachutes and stencil these areas light blue. Replace these cutouts once the paint dries.

4 Cut along the lines defining the sections of the parachutes. With a stencil brush and light blue paint shade along these lines by lifting and replacing the cutouts as needed.

5 Cut around the outside of the pigs' bodies and roller stencil these areas a pink fleshtone.

6 Shade around the outside of the pigs' arms, legs, heads, midriffs, and hooves with a darker pink. Replace the cutouts.

7 Cut along the lines that separate the pigs' heads from their arms, and ears from their heads. Similarly cut along the lines that define the pigs' noses and the line that separates the right pig's legs. Shade along these cut lines to distinguish features (see photo for placement of shading).

8 Cut out the pigs' inner ears, nostrils, and mouths and stencil these deep pink.

9 Cut out the pigs' eyes and stencil them brown.

10 Cut around the pigs' shorts and stencil them light brown. Shade around the outside edges of the shorts with brown paint. Replace these cutouts.

11 Cut along the line defining the shorts legs of the right pig and shade along this line with brown paint.

12 Cut out the pockets in the shorts and stencil them brown.

13 Cut out the pigs' shirts (including their harnesses). Stencil one green and the other blue. Shade around the outside edge of the green shirt with dark green and the outside of the blue shirt with dark blue. Replace the shirt cutouts.

14 Cut out the harnesses and stencil them yellow.

15 With a stylus (or something similar) place marks on the wall through the freezer paper where the parachute lines meet to form Ys.

16 Remove all the freezer paper and use a yardstick and a gray paint pen to paint the parachute lines. The stylus marks will act as a guide for your line placement.

17 With a stencil brush and a little pink paint, add some rose shading to the pigs' cheeks.

Puppy Love

IF YOU AREN'T allowed to get a puppy, then get eight! These pups are so adorable that you won't be able to pick one over the other, so you might as well take the whole litter. Potty-trained and kid-friendly, they are a welcome addition to any room of the house.

If you want to place these puppies along a baseboard in your house, I recommend applying your sprayed freezer paper to the wall at a comfortable height for working on and tracing your image. Once your image is traced, lower the paper so your design will appear at baseboard level and do your cutting and painting there. These puppies would also make a great wall border along the top of a play table.

Method

1 Cut out all around the outside of the puppies and remove this large cutout, saving it for replacement later. If your wall is not white, roller stencil this exposed area white.

2 Use a stencil brush to shade with medium gray paint all around the inside edge of this cutout area.

3 Replace the paper cutout. Cut along the small lines separating the puppies' toes. Using medium gray paint, and a small stencil brush to shade between the toes, lifting and replacing toes as you go. See photo for shading details.

4 Cut out around the gray and brown sections of the heads. (These sections contain eyes and eyebrows – do not

cut around them at this time.) Remove the brown sections, stencil them and replace their cutouts. Remove the gray cutouts, and similarly stencil their openings and replace their cutouts. When the paint dries replace the cutouts.

5 Cut along the lines seperating the puppies' ears from their faces, and use linear shading to shade along these lines (see linear shading page 88). Check the photo for placement of the shading.

6 Cut out all the light gray and medium gray sections, cutting them as one piece where light gray and medium gray pieces meet. Before removing these pieces number them for easy placement later, unless you just love jigsaw puzzles!

7 Roller stencil these areas light gray. Shade under the dogs' chins with a little medium gray.

8 When the light gray paint dries, replace the cutouts.

9 Cut out the medium gray areas and stencil them. You will be stenciling medium gray over the light gray.

10 Cut out the black portions of the puppies' noses, leaving the white spot stuck to the wall. Stencil the noses black.

11 Cut out the puppies' eyes and stencil them black. Use the end of a stencil brush dipped in white paint to dab a spot of white in each of the puppies' eyes.

12 Cut out the puppies' eyebrows and stencil them light gray.

13 Remove all the freezer paper.

All Nite Café

FRASIER MEETS SEINFELD in this lighthearted mural that features a Seattle nightscape as seen through the window of an all night café. Turn out the lights and the neon sign really gets into the act. It glows in the dark!

Cautionary Note to Parents: Décor of this nature may have its drawbacks. Your "baby" may still be living at home long after his teenage years.

SPECIAL TOOLS AND MATERIALS

- White, dark violet, and dark dusty purple paint
- Water-based glaze
- Paint tinted darker than the wall color (or shadow glaze)
- Paint tinted lighter than the wall color
- Five stencil rollers (or one roller and four refills)
- Yellow and pink glow-in-the-dark paint
- Paint pens in red and yellow
- Painter's tape
- Pencil
- Ruler

Method

1 Cut out the window opening, excluding the windowsills and casings.

2 If your wall is not white, roller stencil this opening white using eggshell or semi-gloss paint. Use the dry roller technique around the edge to prevent paint from bleeding under the paper. It will probably take several coats of paint to get adequate coverage.

3 Once the paint dries, roll on a coat of dark violet glaze (one part paint to four parts water-based glaze) to achieve a translucent night sky.

4 Allow adequate drying time for the glaze, as glazes take longer to dry than paint. You may speed up this process by using a hairdryer. Replace the window opening cutout once the glaze is dry.

5 Cut out the windowsill. Stencil it a lighter tint than the wall color. Save the cutout for replacement later.

6 Cut out the top window casing and the left window casing and save the cutouts. Roller stencil these with shadow glaze or with paint tinted darker than the wall color. When dry, draw a line with a ruler and pencil where the top casing meets the left casing.

7 Replace the window casing and windowsill cutouts.

8 Cut out along the Seattle skyline and remove the bottom cutout. Roller stencil this area a dark dusty purple.

9 When the purple paint dries, replace the   skyline cutout.

10 Cut out the pink portions of the neon sign with the exception of the pink border, and use a stencil brush to stencil these areas white.

11 Once the white paint dries, stencil these same areas with glow-in-the-dark fluorescent pink paint. Similarly, cut out the yellow sections of the sign, and stencil them white before top-coating them with glow-in-the-dark yellow paint.

12 Remove the freezer paper from the wall, and use painter's tape to define the pink neon border for stenciling.

The painter's tape will leave you with square corners, so be sure to round these before stenciling. To round the corners, first fill them in with painter's tape. The tape will act as stencil paper. Use a small cylinder such as a spice jar to trace a curved pattern on the tape for cutting and stenciling.

13 Remove all the painter's tape. To make your neon sign even more dramatic, trace around the outside of the yellow portions with a yellow paint pen and around the outside of the pink sections with a red paint pen.

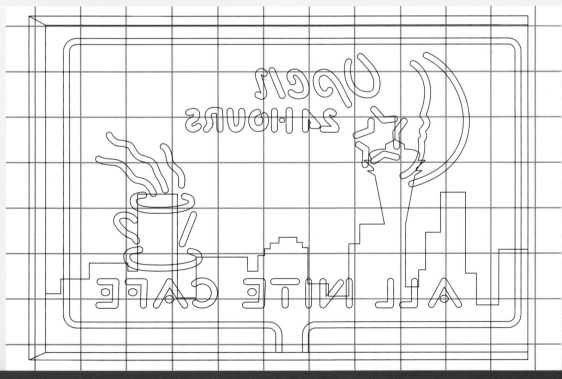

Out of Africa

GEORGINA KING AND I, for an episode of Debbie Travis' TV show "The Painted House," painted this panoramic mural in the children's playroom of the Gilda Radner House in Montreal. Using projection stenciling techniques, we took the stark basement room and turned it into a vast African savanna filled with zebras, elephants, giraffes, flamingos, and a hippopotamus. The center was opened a few days later, and children's laughter completed the picture.

We painted this mural in two stages. In the first stage we set the scene by painting the background hills, fields, pond, and acacia trees. In the second stage we added the wildlife. The instructions are written so you can paint the setting first and then add the animals one at a time, placing them where they look best in your own room.

Setting

1 Basecoat the wall pale warm yellow, and allow several days' drying time. The basecoat becomes the sky in your mural.

2 Cover the wall with freezer paper and trace the background hills, distant fields, pond, and large acacia trees and their shadows.

3 Cut along the top of the most distant hills, cutting through the trees as you go. Lift the top of the cut line slightly and using a dry brush stenciling technique, rub a little pink along the bottom cut edge creating a sunset glow.

4 Cut along the bottom of the distant hill (again cutting straight through the trees) and remove this long cutout. Roller stencil this opening light hazy purple. When the paint dries, replace the cutout.

5 Cut along the base of the treed purple hill and along the line dividing the distant field from the foreground field. Remove this cutout and stencil its opening medium golden yellow. When the paint dries, replace the cutout.

6 Cut along the top of the purple hill, following the outlines of the small trees as you cut. Remove this cutout and stencil the opening purple.

7 Cut around the pond, but don't remove the cutout. Flip up the top edge of the freezer paper where the marsh grass meets the water and with a large

SPECIAL TOOLS AND MATERIALS

- Paint: pale warm yellow, pink, light hazy purple, purple, light golden yellow, medium golden yellow, deep olive green
- One large stencil brush
- Five stencil rollers (or one roller and four refills)

stencil brush, shade along this edge with light hazy purple. Cut out the openings in the grass and shade them purple. Do these openings one at a time so you can replace each cutout as you go.

8 Carefully remove the large cutout representing the foreground field. Leave the "water," including the openings in the grass, stuck to the wall. Save the portions of the freezer paper containing the large acacia trees. Roller stencil the field light golden yellow.

9 Once the paint dries, reposition the acacia trees on the wall. Cut out the shadows of the trees and stencil them with shadow glaze (one part raw umber paint to three parts glaze). Replace the shadow cutouts when the glaze dries.

10 Cut out the large acacia trees and stencil them deep olive green.

11 Remove all the freezer paper.

Wildlife

Populate the savanna with zebras, elephants, giraffes, flamingos, and hippos. Project your images and trace them on freezer paper where you wish them to appear in your mural.

Elephants

1 Cut out the shadows of the elephants and roller stencil them with shadow glaze. When the glaze dries, replace the cutout.

2 Cut out around the outside of the elephants and remove the cutout. Roller stencil the opening light gray. With medium gray paint, shade around the outside of the elephant's bodies where the light gray meets the background field. See the photo for shading placement. Replace the cutout once the paint dries.

3 Cut out the elephant's tusks and stencil them white. Replace the cutouts.

4 Cut out around the outside of the light gray areas and leave them and the tusks stuck to the wall while you remove the other sections. Roller stencil the exposed areas medium gray and replace the cutouts once the paint dries.

5 Cut out the dark gray areas and roller stencil them dark gray.

SPECIAL TOOLS AND MATERIALS

- Paint: light gray, white, medium gray, dark gray
- Shadow glaze (one part raw umber paint, three parts water-based glaze)
- One large stencil brush
- Four stencil rollers (or one roller and three refills)

Flamingos

1 Cut out around the outside of the flamingos' bodies, and remove the cutouts. Roller stencil the flamingos pale pink.

2 Using a stencil brush, shade around the outside of the flamingos' bodies with medium pink. Replace the cutouts when the paint dries.

3 Cut out the dark pink sections of the birds (including the eyes) and stencil these sections deep pink. Replace the cutouts in the wing and tail once the paint dries.

4 Cut out the medium pink sections of the birds and roller stencil them medium pink.

Hippopotamus

1 Cut out around the outside of the hippopotamus' body and remove the cutout. Roller stencil the hippo light mud gray and use a stencil brush to shade along his back and the outside edge of his bottom lip. When the paint dries, replace the cutout.

2 Cut out all the shaded gray sections and remove. Where light and dark shaded sections are adjacent, remove the cutout as one piece. Save the cutouts that have dark shaded sections as part of them. Roller stencil the openings medium mud gray. Replace the cutouts that have dark gray areas on them.

3 Cut out the dark gray sections and roller stencil them dark gray.

SPECIAL TOOLS AND MATERIALS

FLAMINGOS
- Paint: pale pink, medium pink, dark pink
- One large stencil brush
- Three stencil rollers (or one roller and two refills)

HIPPOPOTAMUS
- Paint: light mud gray, medium mud gray, dark gray
- One large stencil brush
- Three stencil rollers (or one roller and two refills)

Giraffes

1 Cut out the giraffes' silhouettes and roller stencil them deep hazy purple.

SPECIAL TOOLS AND MATERIALS
• Paint: deep hazy purple
• One stencil roller

Zebras

1 Cut out the shadows of the zebras and roller stencil them with shadow glaze. Replace this cutout when the glaze dries.

2 Cut out around the outside of the zebras' bodies and remove these large cutouts. Roller stencil the openings white.

3 With a large stencil brush shade around the outside of the zebras' bodies. When the paint dries, replace the cutouts.

4 Cut out the black sections of the zebras and roller stencil them black.

SPECIAL TOOLS AND MATERIALS
• Paint: white, gray, black (I added a little blue to the black)
• Shadow glaze (one part raw umber paint to three parts water-based glaze)
• Three stencil rollers (or one roller and two refills)